George.
One day in the tropical rain
forest.

One Day in the Tropical Rain Forest

The Cry of the Crow
Going to the Sun
The Grizzly Bear with the Golden Ears
Julie of the Wolves
My Side of the Mountain
One Day in the Alpine Tundra
One Day in the Desert
One Day in the Prairie
One Day in the Woods
Shark Beneath the Reef
The Summer of the Falcon
The Talking Earth
Water Sky
The Wild, Wild Cookbook
The Wounded Wolf

One Day in the Tropical Rain Forest

BY JEAN CRAIGHEAD GEORGE

ILLUSTRATED BY GARY ALLEN

Thomas Y. Crowell   New York

One Day in the Tropical Rain Forest
Text copyright © 1990 by Jean Craighead George
Illustrations copyright © 1990 by Gary Allen

Library of Congress Cataloging-in-Publication Data
George, Jean Craighead, date
  One day in the tropical rain forest / by Jean Craighead George ;
illustrated by Gary Allen.
      p.   cm.
  Includes bibliographical references.
  Summary: The future of the Rain Forest of the Macaw depends on a
scientist and a young Indian boy as they search for a nameless
butterfly during one day in the rain forest.
  ISBN 0-690-04767-3 : $ — ISBN 0-690-04769-X (lib. bdg.) :
$
  1. Human ecology—Juvenile literature.   2. Rain forest ecology—
Juvenile literature.   3. Human ecology—Venezuela—Juvenile
literature.   4. Rain forest ecology—Venezuela—Juvenile literature.
5. Deforestation—Venezuela—Juvenile literature.   [1. Rain forest
ecology.   2. Jungle ecology.   3. Ecology.]   I. Allen, Gary (Gary
J.), ill.   II. Title.
GF54.5.G46 1990   89-36583
508.315'2—dc20   CIP
                                                        AC

1 2 3 4 5 6 7 8 9 10
First Edition
JUL 16 '90

To My
Granddaughter
Katie

May there always be scarlet macaws,
and orchids, and cebus monkeys,
and prehensile-tailed porcupines,
and army ants, and great kiskadees,
and jaguars, and unknown butterflies,
for you and your friends.

One Day in the Tropical Rain Forest

Tepui, a slender Indian boy, rolled out of his hammock in a round thatched hut in a Venezuelan forest. He picked up his blowgun, darts in a quiver, and his pack. Tiptoeing past his sleeping parents, he found his bow and two arrows. Quietly he left his hut in a village on the banks of the Orinoco River. He hurried to the state road and strode off along it. It was 6:29 A.M., the moment of sunrise.

Tepui and his people lived in a tropical rain forest, a community of interlocking parts as complex and miraculous as life itself.

On this day, as every day, a number of the parts began to act upon each other in the grand plan of life in the tropical rain forest.

6:45 A.M.

• Tepui left the dirt road and entered the Tropical Rain Forest of the Macaw. He walked on a well-worn footpath called the Trail of the Potoo. It was named for a bird that puts its beak up in the air when it is sitting still. In this pose it is hard to tell the big bird from a tree stub.

• Under the trunk of a fallen tree miles ahead of Tepui, a jaguar opened her eyes. She had black rosettes on yellowish-brown fur, and a massive head, shoulders, and forefeet. She was listening to a frightening sound.

• A colony of vicious army ants, one million strong, crackled as the ants stirred like a pot of boiling water in their bivouac between two rocks.

• Not far from the ants two beetles the size of baseballs tapped the ground with their forefeet and clanged their finger-sized pincers. They were the tropical rain forest's gigantic Hercules beetles, and they resembled knights in armor.

• Near the beetles, a soldier termite entered a tunnel into his colony's nest, a large roundish blob on the side

3

of a tree. The black, hard nest was made of chewed wood cemented with termite fecal glue. The soldier closed the tunnel by plugging it with his large head. His gunlike snout was pointed outward. Through it he could shoot a noxious chemical at the birds and beasts that eat termites. He sat still. The night's battles were over, the day's defense work was beginning.

• Uphill from the termites, a butterfly split the hard outer coat of her chrysalis and poked a foot into the warm, damp air. She had no name.

• Not far from her the elegant great kiskadee whistled two melodious notes, flew out, caught a moth, and flew back to his perch.

• The treetop birds awoke and flashed their brightly colored feathers. Yellow orioles, blue and yellow, and green, blue, black, and red tanagers preened their wings and flew. Purple honeycreepers, blue fruit-eaters, iridescent hummingbirds, and multicolored toucans, and wood warblers flew through the top limbs of the forest.

• A scarlet macaw hooked her beak on a vine and

pulled herself abreast of her last year's nest. She looked into a dark deep hole in the tallest tree in the Tropical Rain Forest of the Macaw. Spring was coming, and it was time to clean her nest. The big parrot was mostly red. Her lower back and outer tail feathers were bright blue. Yellow feathers tipped with green gleamed on her wings. She opened them. They spread three feet from tip to tip. When she flew, she looked like a fiery meteor. Below her a flock of orange-winged parrots began to chatter. A pair of blue and green parakeets touched beaks in a bower of silver webbing. It had been spun during the night by a busy spider. Like the millions of other webs draped through the forest, this one sparkled with raindrops.

The mate of the scarlet macaw called to her, and she joined him on the flight to the cashew trees along the Orinoco River. Thirty other macaws joined them, streaking the sky red as they flew off to eat.

• Above the macaw nest hole a three-toed sloth hung on the underside of a branch. A baby clung to her chest. He poked his head out of her fur, on which mosslike algae grew. The baby snorted. His eyes were large and scrunched close to his nose and mouth. The fuzzy infant's face looked very much like a turtle's.

The mother was an apartment house. In her long fur lived not only plants but some ninety little creatures. Among the tenants were pretty sloth moths, glossy beetles, and numerous pink or white mites. None could survive anywhere but on a sloth in a tropical rain forest. They were stirring. This was a big day for the tenants. The sloth was going to make her weekly trip to the floor of the forest, and they, of course, were going with her.

• In another tree a little capuchin monkey, who was almost a year old, unwrapped her tail from around a limb and wrapped it around her mother, who rubbed her own tummy and yawned.

• Ahead of Tepui in the Science Laboratory of the Tropical Rain Forest, a lanky scientist swung out of his hammock and stretched. Dr. Juan Rivero was one of five biologists who were studying the plants and animals of the forest before it was destroyed.

This day, the twenty-first day of January, was doomsday for the Tropical Rain Forest of the Macaw. Eleven bulldozers and four trucks carrying twenty chain sawyers were rumbling along. For days they had been moving down the highway from the city of Caracas on the hills above the Gulf of Mexico. The ominous caravan was headed for the state of Monagas and Tepui's tropical rain forest. Its mission was to cut down and burn the vines, flowers, and trees and to ready the land for crops.

The forest was home to millions of species of wild plants and animals. Many had never been seen by human eyes. The tangle of plants hid unknown creatures in the bracts and corollas of flowers, in the shelter of hollow and twisted stems, and under the curls of bark and leaf buds. For their part, the animals hid unknown plants in dens and nests, and even in their fur.

Although the tropical rain forests of the world lie only between the Tropic of Cancer and the Tropic of Capricorn, they are vital to the health of the entire Earth. They breathe out oxygen. They remove from the atmosphere the polluting carbon dioxide thrown off by automobiles, fires, and industrial plants. This airborne carbon is destructive. It holds in the Earth's heat like the glass of a greenhouse, warming the land, sea, and air. Deserts grow bigger, the ice caps melt, and oceans rise. If for no other reasons than these, the approaching death of the Tropical Rain Forest of the Macaw would be a tragedy; but there are other reasons, as well.

The tropical rain forests are so old, they felt tremors when the Sierra Nevada mountains were uplifted. And they are so young that new species are even now evolving in their warmth and moisture from Central and South America to Africa, from Madagascar and the East Indies to Australia.

7:00 A.M.

Tepui's long legs moved rhythmically as he walked and listened to the chime of the night's rainwater dropping through as many as ten understories of trees growing beneath the 120-foot-high forest canopy. The rainwater splashed onto the shrub layer of ferns and bluish-leafed plants that grow in the near-darkness at

9

the bottom of the forest, then seeped into the fallen leaves on the ground. It leached out their nutrients. Laden, the water sank into the thin soil. Roots absorbed it and sent it back up to feed the leaves and flowers. The recycling was swift. The fallen leaves of the tropical rain forest do not have time to decay and form deep soil, as they do in the forests of North America. There is no winter rest period here. The plants are constantly working.

7:30 A.M.

The humidity rose. The leg and body joints of the army ants moved more freely. They left their bivouac and fanned out forty feet across the ground like a river of tar. Before them raced a cloud of the terrified insects they feed upon. The thousands of fleeing crickets, katydids, and beetles roared like a chain saw.

They buzzed over the jaguar's den, warning her of what was to come. With a sharp *merrow* she told her cubs to follow her. One had an infected paw. He limped from under the fallen tree. As large as the jaguar and her cubs were, they were no match for a million flesh-eating ants.

7:45 A.M.

Tepui passed beneath a giant tree. It measured ten feet across its fluted base and reached up above the canopy. Only a few species of trees in the rain forest grow to such heights, and of these, only a few individuals manage to pierce the canopy. The competition for sunlight in this jungle of warmth and moisture is ferocious. A plant victory can take centuries.

One tree, a Coco de Mono, was Tepui's favorite, and larger than all the others. It was 150 feet tall and growing. Vines, orchids, moss, ferns, bromeliads, grew over and upon it. Lizards, snakes, leaf-cutting ants, wasps, beetles, and frogs ate, slept, and lived out their lives upon it. Opossums, porcupines with prehensile tails like hands, silky anteaters, and bats visited the tree. Colorful birds came to nest, feed, and rest in its niches. Some drilled holes in its trunk. At the bottom of the tree bright-red land crabs hid from the crab-eating raccoons.

11

Two long-nosed tapirs grazed its plants, and a white-tailed deer resting beside it got up and ran when an ocelot growled. At the top of the tree small white and yellow flowers burst into bloom in the sunlight. Tepui was headed for this tree.

8:00 A.M.

The eleven bulldozers and four trucks carrying twenty chain sawyers crossed the Monagas state border.

Tepui arrived at the Science Laboratory, where Dr. Rivero and the four other natural scientists not only worked but lived. They shared the moist, dark rooms with mosses, ferns, house wrens, and begonias. The plants and animals of the jungle do not know about human property rights. What space they find is theirs.

Tepui had been hired as an assistant by the scientists. He knew where the birds nested and the mammals played. He knew where the reptiles sunned and the amphibians crawled. The rain forest was his hometown, and he was its enthusiastic mayor.

Like a good mayor Tepui introduced the visitors to

13

the residents. He showed the ornithologist a nest of a black-tailed trogon, who has a startling bright-green chest and a crimson belly. He showed him falcons and hawks, vultures and nightjars. He took him to a tree where the toucans daintily plucked red fruit with their big, awkward-looking, five-inch-long bills, almost as long as their bodies.

He introduced the herpetologist to a twelve-foot boa constrictor and a deadly poisonous fer-de-lance snake.

One day he brought him a marsupial frog, who carries her eggs in a watery sac on her back. Before their eyes the eggs changed into polywogs. A few days later the polywogs turned into frogs, and the frogs hopped off their mother's back like clowns from a car in a circus act. The herpetologist laughed as he took notes and counted frogs.

On one occasion Tepui took the mammalogist to the nest of the elusive marsupial mouse, who carries her babies in a pocket like the kangaroo. He led her to the lair of a tayra, or weasel, and found her a family of agoutis, rodents with long ears and legs that look like a

cross between a rabbit and a deer. At night he showed her vampire bats cruising the forest in search of sleeping mammals to feed upon. With a flashlight he showed her the littlest cat of the jungle, the pretty margay. There were no wolves to show the mammalogist, for wolves never lived in this part of South America, even eons ago. But he did show her a family of peccaries, or wild pigs.

At one time Tepui brought the mammalogist a mischievous baby capuchin monkey. The smart little girl monkey learned to open boxes more quickly than the mammalogist. She invented dishes by mixing bowls of cornflakes with boxes of paper clips. She carried gifts of flowers to the mammalogist, but when she brought a dead mouse to the botanist, Tepui returned her to her tribe.

Tepui also helped the botanist. He found her plants that she did not know existed on this earth. He showed her trees that suddenly rained down leaves. There is no autumn in the tropical rain forest, but the trees do shed their leaves. Some individual trees have their

own sudden autumns, and Tepui knew that moment for many of them.

Tepui made the men and women at the laboratory extremely happy; all, that is, but Dr. Juan Rivero, the lepidopterist. Although Tepui had brought him the incredible transparent butterfly that casts no shadow, it did not make him happy. Tepui captured for him sunset-yellow swallowtails and fritillaries, copper and orange angle-winged butterflies. He found metalmarks; skippers; brush-footed and gossamer-winged butter-flies. But—he could not find what the man really wanted: a butterfly that no one had seen or named before.

If Dr. Rivero could find a nameless butterfly, a wealthy industrialist would buy the Tropical Rain Forest of the Macaw, name the butterfly for his daughter, and save the forest from the bulldozers and chain sawyers.

Months had passed, and Tepui had not found a nameless butterfly for Dr. Rivero.

8:15 A.M.

The bulldozers and trucks stopped. The woodsmen climbed to the ground and bought fresh papaya juice at a roadside stand. They drank in the cool shade of an acacia tree.

The air was very still when Tepui arrived at the laboratory. The nine-foot-long fronds of the fern trees that usually dance and leap were as motionless as paintings. Tropical dragonflies hovered above them like crystal airplanes, and brilliant hummingbirds flashed their metallic colors around them.

"Good morning, Tepui," Dr. Rivero said.

"Good morning," Tepui replied in Spanish learned at the mission school not far from his village.

"Today is our last chance to save the forest," Dr. Rivero's voice was grave. His bearded jaw drooped like the chin of a capybara, South America's biggest rodent. "The bulldozers and chain sawyers are on their way."

"Then today must be the day," said Tepui. "I have a plan." He put down his blowgun, which he always

19

carried for protection, and held up his bow and arrows. Dr. Rivero shook his head. Bows and arrows did not interest him. They could not catch nameless butterflies.

Tepui stepped off the porch. Taking a bearing on the tallest tree in the rain forest, he led Dr. Rivero off along the Trail of the Potoo.

9:00 A.M.

The bulldozer drivers, truck drivers, and chain sawyers got back in their vehicles and rolled again.

9:30 A.M.

The butterfly shook fluid into her wings, and they opened like flower petals. Iridescent purple "eyes" appeared in a metallic-blue field on her forewings. On her hindwings a white and blue checkerboard emerged on a background of green-gold. Sequins could not have sparkled more tantalizingly than the wings of the nameless butterfly.

The man and the boy walked in deep shadow. The plants of the rain forest battle each other for sunlight.

20

War is always going on among them, and to win they have invented ingenious ways to fight. The fig actually strangles: A fig seedling in a palm tree had sent a long root to the ground. It was sending down others. They would grow together, surround the palm, cut off the light, and kill it.

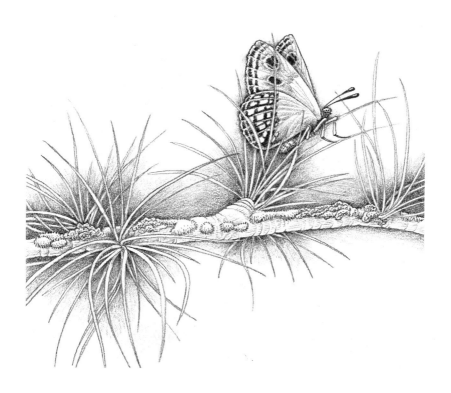

Most orchids and bromeliads abandoned the struggle for light on the ground and moved up onto the limbs of trees. There they take nourishment from the rain they catch in the bases of their leaves and from the soil their dead leaves build up on the huge limbs.

The woody liana vines loop and twist to the light like snakes. They find a spot of sun, wrap a tendril, put out leaves, and reach for another sun spot. A single vine will travel miles through the trees, devouring light. The loops and drapes woven by the many different kinds of vines have become the hallmark of the tropical rain forest.

10:00 A.M.

The sloth began her trip to the ground. Her tenants were ready. They moved to the ends of fur tufts facing down.

The eleven bulldozers and four trucks carrying twenty chain sawyers rolled on toward the Tropical Rain Forest of the Macaw.

The jaguar stopped along the Trail of the Potoo and

listened for the marauding ants. The army was not far behind her. It was crossing a gulley by making a bridge of ants holding on to ants holding on to ants. She heard the death scream of a baby crab-eating raccoon and hurried on. One cub trotted at her side, the other limped behind.

10:10 A.M.

The eleven bulldozers and four trucks carrying twenty chain sawyers stopped by a lake to cool off in the shade. Although it was very hot, the men did not swim. The lake was home to thousands of flesh-eating piranhas.

10:15 A.M.

The three-toed sloth reached the ground. With her stubby tail she slowly dug a shallow depression. Into it she defecated, then urinated. No sooner had she completed her weekly ritual than the moths and beetles jumped off her fur and laid eggs in the rich fecal matter. The sloth lifted her forearms and grasped the tree. As she pulled herself up, she kicked leaves over the feces, protecting the eggs of her tenants without even knowing it. As she began to climb, a sloth moth hatched on the ground. It flew up, found the sloth, and settled down in her fur for the long ride to the canopy. High up there in the sunlight it would mature, mate, and one day take the long, slow ride to the ground.

10:17 A.M.

The two Hercules beetles met on the Trail of the Potoo. One was six inches long, the other four. The first, larger beetle grabbed the smaller with his huge pincers and lifted him above his head. Walking almost upright, he crossed the trail and hurled his opponent to the ground like a Japanese wrestler. The four-incher landed on his back with a loud crack. His feet flayed piteously as he tried to right himself. While he struggled, the six-incher walked off to court a female. Suddenly he was picked up by a third beetle, who carried him across the trail and hurled him onto his back. The first beetle struggled to his feet and picked up the third beetle.

10:20 A.M.

The army ants flowed out on the Trail of the Potoo and headed uphill toward the jaguar family.

10:22 A.M.

The black horde rolled over the Hercules beetles.

10:25 A.M.

The army moved on. All that remained of the warriors were their empty exoskeletons.

The drivers and sawyers returned to the eleven bulldozers and four trucks. They rolled on toward the Tropical Rain Forest of the Macaw.

10:30 A.M.

The great kiskadee reached up and caught a transparent butterfly.

The sloth, who was halfway between the ground and the lowest limb, stopped to eat some young leaves. She

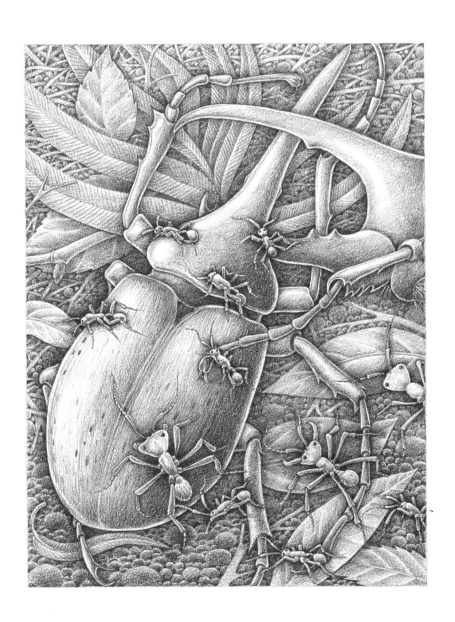

chewed, letting little pieces remain on her lips. The black-eyed baby stuck out his tongue and tasted them. He was only six weeks old and would nurse for another four months, but he was already in sloth school. By tasting leaves on his mother's lips, he would learn what leaves to eat. The mother hung by all four three-toed feet and rested. She would carry the baby against her chest until he was six months old and on his own. Immediately, she would become pregnant again for another six months. The female three-toed sloth carries a baby either inside or outside all her adult life, which begins when she is three years old.

10:31 A.M.

Tepui and Dr. Rivero pushed back the large leaves of a tree of the banana family and the dangling roots of philodendron as they penetrated an overgrown part of the Trail of the Potoo. The fancy bird-of-paradise flowers bloomed along it, and vivid pink impatiens brightened the shade. The air was moist and humid.

10:35 A.M.

The man and boy stopped to rest and cool off not far from the termite nest, now closed for the day by the bodies and heads of the soldiers. In the lightless corridors behind them the caste system was at work. The queen was laying forty-five eggs a minute. The tireless workers were carrying them to the nursery, where they would be cared for by other tireless workers. The soldiers were guarding the nest. The kings, having mated, had disappeared.

The termites, like the rain, recycle the nutrients of the tropical forests. At night they eat dead wood and fallen leaves. Bacteria and protozoans in their guts convert the cellulose into a sugar rich with wood nutrients. When a bird or anteater eats the termites, the nutrients are passed along, eventually getting back to the soil and the trees and flowers.

10:40 A.M.

The eleven bulldozers and four trucks carrying twenty chain sawyers turned onto the dirt road that led to the Tropical Rain Forest of the Macaw and Tepui's village.

The humidity was 90 percent, the temperature 85 degrees Fahrenheit. Clouds suddenly formed. Like ghosts they floated among the trees and vines. The details of the forest faded, leaving only the misty silhouettes of trees. Tepui sniffed the air. "Rain," he said to Dr. Rivero. Since thirty feet of water fall on the tropical rain forest each year, Tepui knew well the smell of rain. Less than four feet fall on lush New England.

The jaguar heard the cloud of terrified insects coming closer. She looked back. One cub was behind her, the other was far away, limping in the darkness before the storm. She waited.

10:43 A.M.

The rain roared down.

Two antbirds who were attacking the termite nest flew to shelter under a banana-type tree.

The great kiskadee stood under an umbrella of leaves on the tallest tree.

Tepui and Dr. Rivero walked on in the rain.

11:00 A.M.

The eleven bulldozers and four trucks carrying twenty chain sawyers came to a halt. A flood from a distant rainstorm rushed across the road. The forest upon which it used to fall had been cut down, and now the rain tore up the soil and avalanched mud slides. The sawyers had to wait for the flood to abate.

11:05 A.M.

The rain stopped. The sun came out. Tepui and Dr. Rivero rounded a bend in the trail and came upon the carcasses of the Hercules beetles.

"Army ants," said Tepui. "The beetles have been recently killed." He peered into the dripping jungle. "The ants are close by. I smell them." Dr. Rivero knew the vicious reputation of these ants that have devoured men sleeping in hammocks, dogs on their leashes, and every other living creature that does not flee them. "Let's get out of here," he said.

30

The voices startled the jaguar. She leaped onto the trail in front of them and crouched to spring. Tepui lifted his blowgun, loaded it with a slender dart, and was about to shoot when the jaguar suddenly twisted to the ground, howling and biting.

"Army ants have her," Tepui shouted.

The jaguar fled into the jungle, rolling and swatting, one cub mewing at her side.

A bloodcurdling yowl sounded on the trail behind Dr. Rivero. Then there was silence.

Tepui ran to the sufferer.

11:10 A.M.

"The army ants are killing a beautiful jaguar cub," he lamented as Dr. Rivero joined him. The scientist was still both shaken and awed by the sight of the big angry cat. He wiped perspiration from his brow.

Although Tepui and Dr. Rivero knew the law of the jungle—one dies that another can live—it was difficult to be a witness to this truth. They turned and went on.

"Ouch," yelled Dr. Rivero. "Ants!"

"Run!" said Tepui. "Knock them off as you run. Scatter them. Without each other they are helpless." He broke into a run himself, knocking ants from his ankles.

11:20 A.M.

The man and the boy stopped running and sat down to rest. They were soaking wet with rain and perspiration, but they did not complain. As the water evaporated, it cooled them. Dr. Rivero took a drink and passed the bottle of water to Tepui, who was thoughtfully contemplating the forest.

"Did you know that if this forest is cut down, my people will get sick and die?"

"Really?"

"My uncle went to work in a rice field. He died in two years."

"What did he die of, Tepui?"

"Boredom. My people die of boredom without the forest. We need to see and think about thousands of creatures each day to be healthy."

"I can understand that."

"The jungle makes us wonder, and that is healthy. See those two little white-capped birds jumping over each other?"

"The manakins?" answered Dr. Rivero. "Yes, I see them. The ornithologist tells me they jump over each other almost all day long. He said that two, sometimes three, males must jump and jump before the female will mate with one."

"That's what I mean," said Tepui. "Isn't that a wonder? I think about them and I'm no longer bored."

11:30 A.M.

Some of the men from the eleven bulldozers and four trucks fell asleep waiting for the floodwaters to abate.

Tepui and Dr. Rivero heard a trumpeting sound. It was as if crazy musicians were blowing across a forest of empty glass bottles.

"Howler monkeys." Tepui pointed to seven reddish-orange monkeys sitting in a nameless hardwood tree. Their mouths were pursed into O's as they sent their voices for miles through the forest.

They were answered by another troop of howlers. As the tribes roared about their territories and warned each other to stay away, they awoke a family of capuchin

monkeys taking a siesta above Tepui. The young monkey who had wrapped her tail around her mother at dawn looked down on the visitors. She recognized Tepui and Dr. Rivero, her friends from the lab. She squealed excitedly and, running on all fours, bracing herself with her tail, went down a limb. Her weight dipped it to the ground just behind Tepui. With a mischievous cry she snatched an arrow. Chittering playfully, she ran a highway of limbs toward the tallest tree in the forest. Tepui ran beneath her shaking his fist.

"Give me my arrow. I need it. I need it," he shouted as she disappeared in the dripping jungle.

The little girl monkey ran up the tallest tree and sat down on the lowest limb, which was seventy-five feet above the ground. She held on to the arrow.

11:40 A.M.

Her mother called. The little monkey dropped the arrow. Bouncing and falling, it glanced off a leaf and lodged itself in the long fur of the three-toed sloth. The sloth did not move. What was one more tenant to her?

12:00 P.M.

The eleven bulldozer drivers and twenty chain sawyers still waited for the flood to abate.

12:30 P.M.

Along the Trail of the Potoo another cloud suddenly poured rain. Leaves and flowers, twigs and tree trunks, became streambeds.

Tepui and Dr. Rivero, water cascading from their heads and shoulders, arrived at the tallest tree in the Tropical Rain Forest of the Macaw.

The nameless butterfly crept to the underside of a leaf.

The jaguar led her remaining cub to a dry cave under the roots of a fallen tree. She licked her burning ant wounds.

The sloth shed the rain like a waterfall, keeping her tenants snug and dry. Her baby slept, and she hung still. Only her lips moved as she chewed, to say she was an animal not a plant. The arrow remained in place.

12:40 P.M.

The rain stopped. The tanagers and flycatchers, the finches and hummingbirds, flew off to hunt. Doves sang over and over and over, a mournful song that sounded like "Pablo, come home. Pablo, come home."

The air had cleared, and Tepui and Dr. Rivero could see to the top of the tree. But they had to lean backward almost at right angles, the tree was so tall. Up in the sunshine flowers were blooming. Where Tepui and Dr. Rivero stood, the great tree had grown huge flanges like cathedral buttresses to hold up its tons of weight. They were fifteen feet wide and twenty feet high. Coming down two of the buttresses were seemingly endless lines of leaf-cutting ants. Each worker carried over her head, like a parasol, a circle of green leaf she had cut. Each took her prize into an underground nest and laid it down in a dark garden. The leaves were not ant food, but were food for a fungus the ants did eat. The process was much like our growing mushrooms.

Fascinated, Dr. Rivero wondered at the ants, then

39

glanced at Tepui. He was opening his pack.

"Are we stopping here?" he asked.

"Yes, sir," he replied. "We are going to climb to the top of the tree. That's where the flowers and butterflies are."

"And how do we do that?" Dr. Rivero asked with a tinge of fear in his voice.

12:45 P.M.

The flood abated. The eleven bulldozers shoved aside the mud, and then they and the four trucks carrying twenty chain sawyers rolled on.

At the same time Tepui took a large ball of cord from his pack. He tied the end to his remaining arrow, put the arrow against his bowstring, and pulled.

The arrow sped straight up, zinged between vines, and whistled past the sloth. It passed over the first big limb, reached its apogee, and fell back to earth. Tepui untied the cord, stuck the arrow through his string pack, then tied a rope to the end of the cord and pulled it up

and over the limb. Next he took a bamboo ladder out of his pack and tied it to the rope. Hauling on the rope, he pulled the ladder up to the limb and secured it. Quickly he climbed to the first orchid-laden limb.

"Come on up," he called to Dr. Rivero. "There are nameless and beautiful things up here."

Dr. Rivero's face brightened. Forgetting his fears, he stepped on the first rung and slowly climbed skyward. Tepui leaned down to encourage him, and his only arrow fell out of his pack and plunged out of sight in the jungle.

"No!" cried Tepui, reaching for it. Without that arrow he could not get Dr. Rivero to the top of the tree. He covered his face with his hands. The fate of the forest was sealed. No nameless butterflies flitted in the lower limbs of the tree. The forest could not be saved. His heart ached for the animals, the plants, and his people.

12:55 P.M.

The eleven bulldozers and four trucks arrived at the

field office of the tree-cutting company and stopped.

Dr. Rivero was abreast of the sloth. Slowly she turned her head, and as she did so, he saw her. He wondered at her fur, her droll black eyes, her lightweight body, and her three-toed feet. Then he saw Tepui's arrow. He could not reach it. Grabbing the nest hole of the scarlet macaw, he pulled himself and the ladder to the sloth. With a quick movement he let go of the hole and snatched the arrow before he swung back. The baby sloth snorted.

12:58 P.M.

Dr. Rivero threw his leg over the limb where the miserable Tepui sat.

"Surprise," he said, holding up the arrow. "Look what the sloth was keeping for us."

Tepui grinned like an Orinoco River crocodile and closed his eyes gratefully.

1:00 P.M.

Tepui pulled up the ladder, then shot his arrow and

string over the next limb, pulled the ladder to it, and climbed it. Dr. Rivero followed. In this manner they moved up four more limbs, then scrambled into the crown of the tree using just their hands and feet.

1:20 P.M.

Tepui and Dr. Rivero had arrived at the top of the largest tree in the forest. Happy as hummingbirds, they looked out over miles and miles of tree flowers blooming in the sun.

Over them floated silver butterflies, metallic-blue-and-purple butterflies, white, orange, green, and yellow butterflies. A river of checkered butterflies flowed past. Crescent spots washed over the big tree like a waterfall.

"Butterflies by the thousands," marveled Dr. Rivero. "I must be in heaven."

He dipped his net into the fluttering rainbow of wings and caught five butterflies. Tepui carefully put the rare creatures in collecting jars. Dr. Rivero dipped for more.

2:00 P.M.

The boss of the tree company handed a map to the foreman of the wood-cutting crew. "Begin cutting here," he said, pointing to the spot on the dirt road where the Trail of Potoo begins. The men got back into their vehicles and drove off.

3:00 P.M.

"No new ones yet," Dr. Rivero said with heartfelt consternation. He dipped again.

3:01 P.M.

The great kiskadee saw the nameless butterfly alight on a flower.

3:01:10 P.M.

The bird darted out to catch and eat it.

3:01:11 P.M.

The nameless butterfly saw the predator and flew to a flower near Dr. Rivero. The bird did not follow. He dared not come so close to a man.

45

3:01:12 P.M.

Dr. Rivero looked at the butterfly. His trained eye noted the iridescent purple spot on the blue forewing, and the white and blue checkerboard on the green-gold hindwing. He scooped.

"Got her," he cried. "Tepui, I have a nameless butterfly." He looked across the treetops. "Tepui, the Tropical Rain Forest of the Macaw is saved."

Tepui bowed his head and shivered with thankfulness. Then, carefully, he put the precious butterfly in a jar and held her up before his face.

"What is her name, sir?" he asked.

"Cercyonis isabella."

"I love her very much."

"And now to get down and call Caracas," said Dr. Rivero, carefully packing this jar. "We must stop the destruction."

3:30 P.M.

Tepui and Dr. Rivero hit the ground and ran. Descending the tree had been easier than climbing, but

not much. In their haste they tore their clothes and scratched their arms, but they paid no attention.

The chain sawyers tied bright ribbons on the first swath of trees to be cut down. The bulldozers lined up behind them to plow up the stumps and smooth the land for crops.

6:15 P.M.

Tepui and Dr. Rivero reached the lab. Dr. Rivero slid through the door, picked up the radiophone, and put in a call to Caracas.

Tepui kept running.

6:50 P.M.

The sun set.

Tepui arrived at the junction of the state road and the Trail of the Potoo. He dashed right out in front of a bulldozer.

"Stop!" he shouted. "Don't cut down the trees. The Tropical Rain Forest of the Macaw has been saved."

The drivers got off their bulldozers; the chain

sawyers lowered their saws and stared at Tepui. The foreman and the boss yelled at him to go away.

6:51 P.M.

Dr. Rivero ran out of the forest.

"You can all go home," he said. "Tomorrow morning the sun will rise on the International Tropical Rain Forest of the Macaw. After that not one tree can be felled—forevermore."

Tepui grinned like a crocodile.

The Indian workers cheered.

The howler monkeys howled.

The sloth did not move.

Overhead flew the flock of scarlet macaws going home for the night. Their scarlet, yellow, blue, and green feathers were fireworks celebrating the day.

Bibliography

Baker, Jeannie. *Where the Forests Meet the Sea*. New York: Greenwillow Books, 1987.

Britannica Junior Encyclopedia. Vol. 14, p. 312. Chicago: Encyclopedia Britannica, 1988.

de Schauensee, Rodolphe Meyer, and William H. Phelps, Jr. *A Guide to the Birds of Venezuela*. Princeton: Princeton University Press, 1978.

Jansen, Daniel H., ed. *Costa Rican Natural History*. Chicago/London: The University of Chicago Press, 1983.

Monastersky, R. "Carbon Dioxide: Where Does It All Go?" *Science News, the Weekly Magazine of Science*, August 26, 1989, vol. 136, no. 9, p. 132.

Perry, Donald R. *Journey into a Hollow Tree*. Hillside, New Jersey: Enslow Publishers, 1980.

Pittaway, Margaret. *The Rainforest Children*. New York: Oxford University Press, 1980.

Reynolds, Jean, ed. *The New Book of Knowledge*. Danbury, Connecticut: Grolier, 1987.

Index

Numbers in *italics* refer to illustrations

53